ExamREVIEW.NET

Intellectual Properties, Trademarks and Copyrights

Contents of this book are fully copyrighted.

Exam topics

Welcome to your comprehensive resource designed to prepare you for the certification exam and enhance your skills as an administrative professional. Whether you are just starting your career or looking to validate your experience and knowledge, this book is tailored to help you succeed in a demanding and evolving role.

In today's competitive job market, certification is more than just a credential; it's a testament to your expertise, dedication, and commitment to professional growth. As a certified administrative assistant, you will stand out to employers, demonstrating that you possess the advanced skills and knowledge necessary to excel in administrative roles. Certification can open doors to career advancement, higher salaries, and increased job security.

This book is structured to cover all key areas of the certification exam. It includes a series of practice questions designed to test your understanding and application of the material. Answers and explanations are provided to help you learn from your mistakes and reinforce your knowledge. The practice questions are modeled after those topics listed on the exam blueprint.

Becoming a certified administrative assistant is a significant achievement that reflects your hard work and dedication. This book is here to support you every step of the way, providing the practice and insights you need to excel. Remember, preparation is the key to success. Dive into the questions, challenge yourself, and emerge as a certified professional ready to advance your career.

John the administrative assistant knows that a business letter:

a) Represents the company's internal communication

b) Represents the company to the outside public

c) Is only for formal occasions

d) Should always be handwritten

Answer: b

Explanation: A business letter is a formal communication tool that represents the company to external parties such as clients, suppliers, and other stakeholders.

John the administrative assistant wants to set clear goals for himself. "I will be more resourceful this year" is an example of:

a) A specific goal

b) A vague goal

c) A measurable goal

d) An achievable goal

Answer: b

Explanation: This goal is vague because it lacks specific criteria that make it measurable and actionable.

True or False: Brainpower is essential for administrative tasks.

a) True

b) False

Answer: a

Explanation: Brainpower, which includes problem-solving and critical thinking skills, is essential for efficiently performing administrative tasks.

John the administrative assistant says that when taking notes for a business meeting he should record the meeting discussions verbatim. True or False?

a) True

b) False

Answer: b

Explanation: Recording meeting discussions verbatim is often unnecessary and impractical. Key points and action items are typically more useful.

True or False: Character implies consistency of behavior traits.

a) True

b) False

Answer: a

Explanation: Character involves consistent and reliable behavior that aligns with one's values and principles.

Which of the following is the correct order for storing files using the consecutive numeric storage method?

a) 22 57 63, 16 58 49, 15 63 45, 14 87 23

b) 14 87 23, 15 63 45, 16 58 49, 22 57 63

c) 16 58 49, 14 87 23, 22 57 63, 15 63 45

d) 15 63 45, 22 57 63, 14 87 23, 16 58 49

Answer: b

Explanation: The consecutive numeric storage method arranges files in ascending numeric order.

True or False: Self-discipline is an attitude.

a) True

b) False

Answer: a

Explanation: Self-discipline involves maintaining control and adhering to personal or professional standards, reflecting one's attitude towards consistency and goal achievement.

Cross-functional teams:

a) Are composed of individuals from a particular department

b) Have a matrix structure

c) Are usually permanent teams

d) Are composed of individuals from various departments

Answer: d

Explanation: Cross-functional teams consist of members from different departments working together towards a common goal.

True or False: If you believe you are a victim of sexual harassment at work, file a formal complaint in writing with your organization.

a) True

b) False

Answer: a

Explanation: Filing a formal complaint in writing is a crucial step in addressing sexual harassment and ensuring proper documentation and response.

True or False: While the executive is traveling, you should either handle all matters yourself or refer them to someone else in the company.

a) True

b) False

Answer: b

Explanation: Not all matters can be handled personally or referred; it's important to follow the executive's instructions or organizational protocols.

John the administrative assistant knows the correct order for the steps to follow when introducing oneself. Such order should be:

a) 2, 4, 1, 3

b) 1, 2, 3, 4

c) 4, 3, 2, 1

d) 3, 1, 2, 4

Answer: a

Explanation: The correct order for introducing yourself is to smile and establish eye contact, greet the person and state your name and position, shake hands, and then repeat the person's name.

To verify that all the items received are the items you ordered, John the administrative assistant should compare the packing slip and items received with the:

a) Invoice

b) Sales order

c) Purchase order

d) Delivery receipt

Answer: c

Explanation: The purchase order lists the items ordered and is the document used to verify that the received items match what was ordered.

True or False: Gestures and other nonverbal behaviors cannot send a message.

a) True

b) False

Answer: b

Explanation: Nonverbal behaviors, including gestures, can convey significant messages and often supplement or replace verbal communication.

True or False: Teams in an organization are rarely used but are effective.

a) True

b) False

Answer: b

Explanation: Teams are frequently used in organizations as they can effectively leverage diverse skills and perspectives to achieve goals.

True or False: The accuracy and efficiency of tracking physical records can be improved using bar codes.

a) True

b) False

Answer: a

Explanation: Barcodes help in accurately tracking and managing physical records, enhancing both efficiency and reliability.

True or False: Vertical drawer cabinets are the traditional storage cabinet for physical records.

a) True

b) False

Answer: a

Explanation: Vertical drawer cabinets are a common and traditional choice for storing physical records.

True or False: Although women have made great strides in equal employment, inequalities still exist.

a) True

b) False

Answer: a

Explanation: Despite significant progress, gender inequalities in the workplace persist.

Kay is the team member who offers ideas and suggestions that help the team keep moving. Her informal role is:

a) Facilitator

b) Recorder

c) Initiator

d) Harmonizer

Answer: c

Explanation: The initiator is the team member who suggests new ideas and keeps the team progressing.

True or False: A printed memo should be used (rather than an email) when the information is confidential or sensitive.

a) True

b) False

Answer: a

Explanation: Printed memos can be more secure for sensitive information as they are less prone to digital breaches.

True or False: Most businesses can continue to operate indefinitely even if they do not make a profit.

a) True

b) False

Answer: b

Explanation: Businesses need to make a profit to sustain operations, pay expenses, and invest in growth.

What should leaders model to encourage an open, cooperative, and collaborative environment?

a) Authority

b) Openness

c) Assertiveness

d) Independence

Answer: b

Explanation: Leaders should model openness to foster a culture of cooperation and collaboration within their teams.

To visually represent a problem, help clarify points, and help yourself see an issue differently, you should use:

a) Spreadsheets

b) Mind mapping

c) Text documents

d) Presentations

Answer: b

Explanation: Mind mapping is a visual tool that helps in organizing information and exploring problems from different angles.

True or False: How you express yourself influences the confidence others have in you.

a) True

b) False

Answer: a

Explanation: Clear and confident communication can significantly impact how others perceive your credibility and competence.

True or False: Copies of receipts are usually submitted to verify amounts for travel expenses.

a) True

b) False

Answer: a

Explanation: Copies of receipts are typically required to verify and substantiate travel expense claims.

Jay the administrative assistant is sorting/arranging incoming mail to deliver to the executive. Which of the following should be first (on top of the stack)?

a) Advertisements

b) Personal and confidential items

c) Invoices

d) Regular correspondence

Answer: b

Explanation: Personal and confidential items are prioritized to ensure timely and secure delivery to the executive.

True or False: Project teams are ongoing teams (their assignment does not end).

a) True

b) False

Answer: b

Explanation: Project teams are formed for specific tasks and disband once the project is completed.

True or False: A consumer who buys a new television is an external customer of an electronics store.

a) True

b) False

Answer: a

Explanation: External customers are individuals or entities that purchase goods or services from a business, such as a consumer buying a television from an electronics store.

An example of a time waster is:

a) Interruptions

b) Other people

c) Disorganization

d) All of the above

Answer: d

Explanation: Time wasters can include interruptions, disorganization, and distractions from other people.

True or False: Technical skills are the ability to apply specialized knowledge and procedures to get a job done.

a) True

b) False

Answer: a

Explanation: Technical skills involve the expertise and knowledge required to perform specific tasks and procedures effectively.

Which of the following is a tax-deferred retirement plan for employees of the XYZ Firm which is a private company ?

a) Roth IRA

b) 401(k) account

c) SEP IRA

d) Traditional IRA

Answer: b

Explanation: A 401(k) account is a tax-deferred retirement savings plan offered by private employers, allowing employees to save and invest a portion of their paycheck before taxes.

Mary the administrative assistant says that when planning a business call, you should be aware of the time zone differences for the caller and the recipient. True or False?

a) True

b) False

Answer: a

Explanation: Being aware of time zone differences ensures that business calls are scheduled at appropriate times for all parties involved.

Once you set your priorities, you should not allow anything to change them. True or False?

a) True

b) False

Answer: b

Explanation: Priorities may need to be adjusted based on changing circumstances and urgent tasks.

True or False: Government projections predict that by 2043, the United States will have no racial minority.

a) True

b) False

Answer: a

Explanation: Projections indicate that by 2043, the U.S. will become a majority-minority nation, with no single racial group being the majority.

To manage relationships at work, Mary the administrative assistant should:

a) Focus only on others' needs

b) Take time to think about yourself

c) Avoid all conflicts

d) Ignore office politics

Answer: b

Explanation: Taking time for self-reflection helps in understanding how to better interact with colleagues and manage work relationships.

True or False: It is a good idea to accessorize your desk at work with a lot of personal items.

a) True

b) False

Answer: b

Explanation: While some personal items can make your workspace comfortable, too many can be distracting and unprofessional.

True or False: Budgets affect managers at all levels of the company, but they typically do not affect other employees.

a) True

b) False

Answer: b

Explanation: Budgets impact all employees, as they influence resources available for projects, salaries, and departmental funding.

To know what you need to accomplish each day and in what order, you should use a:

a) Calendar

b) To Do List

c) Journal

d) Planner

Answer: b

Explanation: A To Do List helps prioritize daily tasks and ensures that important activities are completed in order.

True or False: When meeting with people of different cultures, you should avoid gesturing with your hands.

a) True

b) False

Answer: a

Explanation: Gestures can have different meanings in different cultures, so it's best to avoid them to prevent misunderstandings.

True or False: Many organizations use slideshows or webinars to present information and training over an intranet.

a) True

b) False

Answer: a

Explanation: Slideshows and webinars are common tools for internal training and information dissemination.

An example of poor table etiquette is:

a) Using a fork to eat salad

b) Putting a utensil you are using on the table

c) Cutting food into small pieces

d) Using a napkin

Answer: b

Explanation: Placing a used utensil directly on the table is considered poor etiquette; it should be placed on the plate.

True or False: Nonverbal communication symbols have different meanings from culture to culture.

a) True

b) False

Answer: a

Explanation: Nonverbal symbols can vary widely across cultures, leading to potential misunderstandings.

The first step in planning a message is:

a) Choosing the medium

b) Identifying the objective of the message

c) Drafting the content

d) Considering the audience

Answer: b

Explanation: Identifying the objective sets the foundation for the message's purpose and direction.

True or False: Registered Mail service provides insurance for mailed items.

a) True

b) False

Answer: a

Explanation: Registered Mail offers added security and insurance for valuable items.

True or False: It is acceptable for a leader to use texting language in work email.

a) True

b) False

Answer: b

Explanation: Using texting language in professional emails is inappropriate and can appear unprofessional.

When dealing with customers, you should make eye contact:

a) Rarely

b) Occasionally

c) Frequently

d) Never

Answer: c

Explanation: Frequent eye contact conveys confidence and attentiveness, enhancing customer interactions.

Advocating for employees with upper level management is an example of the leadership skill or strategy of:

a) Delegating tasks

b) Being responsible for others

c) Micromanaging

d) Setting goals

Answer: b

Explanation: Advocating shows responsibility and support for employees' needs and interests.

True or False: The laissez-faire style of leadership is appropriate when employees lack skill in an area.

a) True

b) False

Answer: b

Explanation: Laissez-faire leadership works best with skilled and motivated employees who require little supervision.

An intelligent mobile hotspot is:

a) A portable internet connection

b) Can keep devices connected all the time

c) Can be a smartphone feature

d) All of the above

Answer: d

Explanation: An intelligent mobile hotspot offers portable internet and can be a feature in smartphones, providing constant connectivity.

An electronic receipt that represents the purchase of a seat on a flight is called a(n):

a) Boarding pass

b) Invoice

c) E-ticket

d) Reservation

Answer: c

Explanation: An e-ticket is an electronic receipt for a flight purchase, used instead of a paper ticket.

True or False: As an administrative assistant, you may be authorized to answer routine requests for information addressed to the executive.

a) True

b) False

Answer: a

Explanation: Administrative assistants often handle routine inquiries to support executives and streamline operations.

Which of the following is an example of an internal communication barrier?

a) Noise

b) Headache

c) Language difference

d) Cultural difference

Answer: b

Explanation: A headache is a physical condition that can impede effective internal communication.

True or False: The content of a wiki entry can be edited by the person who posted the entry or by the wiki admin but not by others who read the entry.

a) True

b) False

Answer: b

Explanation: Wiki entries can typically be edited by multiple users to ensure collaborative and updated content.

Offering fair and equitable pay is:

a) A legal requirement

b) An ethical way to treat employees

c) Optional for businesses

d) Only important in large companies

Answer: b

Explanation: Fair and equitable pay is an ethical practice that promotes a positive work environment and employee satisfaction.

When you are a job candidate taking part in a team interview, you should:

a) Dominate the conversation

b) Listen carefully to the questions and answer them succinctly

c) Avoid asking questions

d) Focus only on the interviewer

Answer: b

Explanation: Listening and responding succinctly shows respect for the interview process and ensures clear communication.

Electronic slides should:

a) Be full of text

b) Include a title on each slide

c) Use only one color

d) Be animated

Answer: b

Explanation: Titles help organize information and guide the audience through the presentation.

True or False: As a professional, you will probably spend most of your time on tasks that are both urgent and important.

a) True

b) False

Answer: a

Explanation: Urgent and important tasks often take priority in a professional setting, demanding immediate attention and action.

Mary the administrative assistant knows that for employees, belonging to an effective team can result in:

a) More job satisfaction

b) Improved performance

c) A greater likelihood of staying with the company

d) All of the above

Answer: d

Explanation: Effective teams foster job satisfaction, enhance performance, and increase employee retention.

Exercise can:

a) Help reduce stress

b) Improve your mood

c) Boost your energy level

d) All of the above

Answer: d

Explanation: Regular exercise has multiple benefits, including stress reduction, mood improvement, and increased energy levels.

When dealing with customers' concerns, Mary the administrative assistant should offer customers only one solution so they do not become confused. True or False?

a) True

b) False

Answer: b

Explanation: Offering multiple solutions can provide customers with choices and make them feel valued and understood.

True or False: A voucher is a bill from a vendor requesting payment for the items ordered.

a) True

b) False

Answer: b

Explanation: A voucher is a document authorizing payment, while a bill or invoice requests payment.

True or False: Typical office employees, especially managers, spend very little time in meetings.

a) True

b) False

Answer: b

Explanation: Managers often spend a significant amount of time in meetings for planning, coordination, and decision-making.

Which of the following questions should Mary the administrative assistant ask herself when considering the audience for a presentation?

a) Why are the audience members attending the presentation?

b) What knowledge do the audience members already have about the topic?

c) Both A & B

Answer: c

Explanation: Understanding the audience's motivations and existing knowledge helps tailor the presentation to their needs.

True or False: It is appropriate to violate company standards or policies if it means keeping a customer.

a) True

b) False

Answer: b

Explanation: Adhering to company policies ensures consistency and fairness, even if it means losing a customer.

True or False: To observe proper cell phone etiquette, you should turn off your cell phone or turn it on silent in one-on-one interactions and during meetings, classes, and other public events.

a) True

b) False

Answer: a

Explanation: Proper etiquette involves minimizing disruptions by silencing or turning off cell phones in professional and public settings.

True or False: A good, practical rule is to handle a piece of paper only once.

a) True

b) False

Answer: b

Explanation: While handling paper efficiently is important, it may require multiple actions to process it properly.

To record appointments, meetings, assignment due dates, and reminders, Mary the administrative assistant should use a:

a) Journal

b) Planner

c) Calendar

d) Notebook

Answer: b

Explanation: A planner is specifically designed to keep track of appointments, meetings, due dates, and reminders.

True or False: Because of groupthink, it is important for team norms not to be followed.

a) True

b) False

Answer: b

Explanation: While avoiding groupthink is important, team norms should still be followed to ensure cohesion and effectiveness.

True or False: Since social networking sites have privacy settings, it is safe to assume that the images you post will not be seen by future employers.

a) True

b) False

Answer: b

Explanation: Privacy settings are not foolproof, and employers can often access online content; therefore, it's wise to post cautiously.

To help you evaluate the credibility of research sources for a report, you should consider:

a) Who wrote the information

b) Whether the information is current

c) Whether the information is biased

d) All of the above

Answer: d

Explanation: Evaluating the author, currency, and bias of information helps ensure the credibility of research sources.

An example of a time waster at work is:

a) Interruptions

b) Other people

c) Disorganization

d) All of the above

Answer: d

Explanation: Interruptions, disorganization, and distractions from others are common time wasters in the workplace.

A document that lists amounts spent for travel and other business-related items for a specified time period is a(n):

a) Invoice

b) Receipt

c) Expense report

d) Voucher

Answer: c

Explanation: An expense report details the amounts spent on business-related activities over a specific period.

True or False: A letter of application should always be in block letter style.

a) True

b) False

Answer: b

Explanation: While block letter style is common, other professional formats can also be acceptable.

True or False: For alphabetic indexing, all punctuation is considered when indexing personal and business names.

a) True

b) False

Answer: b

Explanation: Punctuation is generally ignored when alphabetically indexing names.

True or False: If a job ad does not give the name of a person, you should use "To Whom it May Concern" as a salutation in your letter of application.

a) True

b) False

Answer: b

Explanation: It's better to use a specific title or department if a person's name is not provided in the job ad.

When sorting/arranging incoming mail to deliver to the executive, which of the following should be on top of the stack?

a) Promotional materials

b) Personal and confidential items

c) Magazines

d) Routine correspondence

Answer: b

Explanation: Personal and confidential items should be prioritized to ensure privacy and prompt attention.

One way of staying motivated is to:

a) Work without breaks

b) Measure your progress

c) Avoid setting goals

d) Focus on others' achievements

Answer: b

Explanation: Measuring progress helps maintain motivation by providing a sense of accomplishment and direction.

True or False: A goal of businesses is to make more money than is spent in operating a business.

a) True

b) False

Answer: a

Explanation: Profitability, or making more money than is spent, is a fundamental goal of most businesses.

True or False: A conference is typically much smaller in scope and has fewer participants than other types of meetings.

a) True

b) False

Answer: b

Explanation: Conferences are usually larger in scope and involve more participants compared to regular meetings.

True or False: It is acceptable for a leader to use texting language in work email.

a) True

b) False

Answer: b

Explanation: Professional communication should avoid texting language to maintain clarity and professionalism.

True or False: Teams in a business setting are not similar in any way to sports teams.

a) True

b) False

Answer: b

Explanation: Both business and sports teams require collaboration, clear roles, and shared goals to be effective.

Employees are motivated by:

a) Money

b) Recognition

c) Interesting work

d) All of the above

Answer: d

Explanation: Multiple factors, including financial incentives, recognition, and engaging work, contribute to employee motivation.

Your attire for a presentation:

a) Should be casual

b) Should be planned out carefully ahead of time

c) Does not matter

d) Should be decided on the day of the presentation

Answer: b

Explanation: Planning attire in advance ensures that you present yourself professionally and appropriately.

The rectangular seating arrangement:

a) Allows the leader to maintain control at the head of the table

b) Encourages informal discussion

c) Is not suitable for large meetings

d) Promotes equality among participants

Answer: a

Explanation: A rectangular seating arrangement positions the leader at the head of the table, facilitating control and focus.

Which of the following printer features allow you to make the copy larger or smaller than the original?

a) Duplex printing

b) Reduction and Enlargement

c) Collating

d) Draft mode

Answer: b

Explanation: Reduction and enlargement features enable the adjustment of the copy size relative to the original document.

Deductions may be made from an employee's pay for which of the following?

a) Income tax

b) Social security tax

c) Medicare tax

d) All of the above

Answer: d

Explanation: Various deductions, including income tax, social security tax, and Medicare tax, are typically taken from an employee's pay.

End of Book

Made in the USA
Las Vegas, NV
03 February 2025

17445694R00050